Are you ready to play I spy? The letters are not in alphabetical order, just like a real game of I spy.

I SPY with my little eye, something beginning with...

Snowman

I SPY with my little eye, something beginning with...

Holly

I SPY with my little eye, something beginning with...

Angel

I SPY with my little eye, something beginning with...

Reindeer

I SPY with my little eye, something beginning with...

Elf

I SPY with my little eye, something beginning with...

Santa Claus

I SPY with my little eye, something beginning with...

Turkey

I SPY with my little eye, something beginning with...

Candy cane

I SPY with my little eye, something beginning with...

Stocking

I SPY with my little eye, something beginning with...

Snow globe

Ornament

I SPY with my little eye, something beginning with...

I SPY with my little eye, something beginning with...

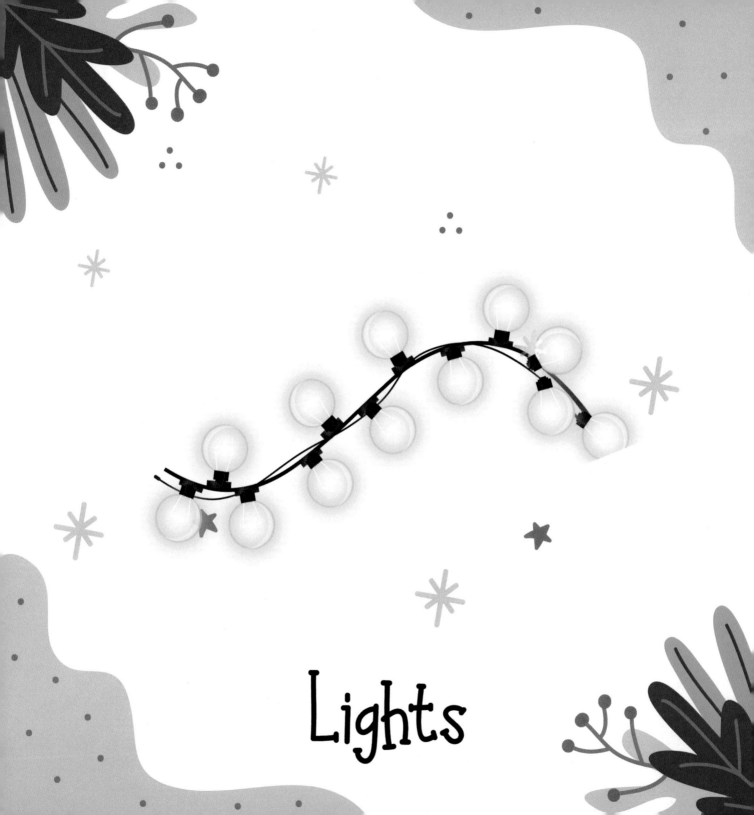

Lights

I SPY with my little eye, something beginning with...

Present Christmas/Gift

I SPY with my little eye, something beginning with...

To:
SANTA CLAUS

Fireplace

I SPY with my little eye, something beginning with...

Candle

I SPY with my little eye, something beginning with...

Bell

I SPY with my little eye, something beginning with...

Wreath

I SPY with my little eye, something beginning with...

Gingerbread

I SPY with my little eye, something beginning with...

Carolers

Made in the USA
Columbia, SC
20 November 2020

25065630R00024